the letters we write

the letters we write

Jamie Papazis

RESOURCE *Publications* · Eugene, Oregon

THE LETTERS WE WRITE

Resource Publications
An Imprint of Wipf and Stock Publishers
199 W. 8th Ave., Suite 3
Eugene, OR 97401

www.wipfandstock.com

PAPERBACK ISBN: 978-1-6667-5090-4
HARDCOVER ISBN: 978-1-6667-5091-1
EBOOK ISBN: 978-1-6667-5092-8

08/04/22

to kathy and gretchen
for not only teaching me how to write
but how to love writing

Contents

i've always hated long prefaces, so i'll make this short and sweet. i wrote this entire collection in the span of two weeks, one lonely february in paris, when i was 19 and studying abroad. i was missing my family, my friends, and the one guy that i had been involved with before moving halfway around the world.

i had written a bit before when i was younger, mostly short stories and the beginning chapters to books i would never finish, but that's how it always was with me. i would have a week or two of inspiration and i would write 10,000 something words, and then the inspiration would leave and i'd get bored, and move on to something else, or be busy with another aspect of my life which allowed no time to write.

but it did allow me to read.

so, words became my way to escape. i'd float through life with taylor swift loud in my earbuds and my nose in a book, drowning out the world. my emotions were understood. life was good. moving to paris threw me for a loop, though. i was in a strange new place, learning a language i didn't speak, and alone. i was utterly alone. so, i held onto the past, onto my friends at home, and onto a relationship that wasn't meant to last. i went through a heartbreak while in the most romantic city in the world. the irony, huh? my complicated, friends-with-benefits relationship was the death of the old jamie—and this book was the birth of the new.

phoenixes always rise from the ashes, don't we?

to him

a letter to him pt i

you are my sun
my moon
my stars
it wrecks my soul
being away from you
missing you more than you will ever know
and knowing you don't miss me at all

you and me

to you
nothing you said
was intentional
it meant nothing
i meant nothing

to me
everything i said
was intentional
it meant everything
you meant everything

waste

i gave you my heart
ripped it out myself
and handed it to you
on a silver platter

you threw it in the trash as you left

polar orbits

i loved him like he was the sun
and i was the moon
destined to come together
and always drift apart

a letter to him pt ii

i have a home in your heart
but not a house
or an apartment—
it's a hotel room
good for one night stands
secret love affairs
and nothing more

i am your escape from reality
you entice me to stay
for the moment
i am what you desire
you need me to stay
for the moment
you crave me
my body is your oasis
my touch is your respite
my voice is your vacation

you tell me as you leave
i should be grateful
for my timeshare in your heart
but in this moment
i feel empty

you didn't care

you dropped my heart
knowing it would shatter

the dark side of the moon

i though you were the sun
but i was wrong
you led me away from the light
dropped my hand
and turned to leave me
in the cold

you would never admit

you love me
you miss me
how much you care

but i think
in your own way
you do

you love me the only way you know how
toasting my bagel to perfection
and remembering i like cinnamon in my hot chocolate

you miss me the only way you know how
wanting me napping in your bed while you work
and showing up at my apartment "just because"

and you care for me the only way you know how
kissing me on the forehead before i leave
and listening to my favorite song in the car

a letter to him pt iii

my heart hurts
it longs for you
feels your presence
everywhere
if i really think
if i close my eyes
i can imagine
your arms
wrapped around me
in a tight embrace
your voice
a whisper
haunting my dreams
your face
on a stranger
in every crowd

art

you took me to the louvre
and told me
i was as pretty as the mona lisa

but while you looked at her
i looked at you

because to me
you were the real masterpiece

fwb

when they ask you
where you got
the things i gave you
do you say they're from me
or do you tell them
they're from a friend

i feel sick to my stomach

thinking about you and her
and how she used to be me

a letter to him pt iv

i am numb
my soul yearns for yours
unequivocally
but unrequited
it is a vise
tightening
around my throat
a hammer
chipping
the first crack
in my heart
it wrecks me
to think about how much
i long for your touch
how much
you consume
my every waking thought
how you even
entwine yourself
in my dreams
and how i know
my memory dares
not even dance
across your mind
for a second
of yours

everywhere

you are everywhere i go
your ghost in the face of a stranger
your laugh carrying across the wind
your voice in the song on the radio
your hands when he touches me

comfort

he feels like a lazy sunday morning
curled up by the fire
with my favorite book
and a cup of tea
while snow drifts down
and frosts the windows

a letter to him pt v

for the first time in my life
as far back as my memory
deigns to reach
the brick wall around my heart
is loosening
your resolve slowly chips away
at my precarious handiwork
and i'm letting it

the walls need to break
the light needs to shine through
so you get to see every piece of my heart
the good
the bad
the happy
the insecure
the moody
the confident
because you won't run

every time
i feel worthless
and attempt to sabotage
the bridge between our hearts
you refuse to let me
when i express
how an action
makes me feel
instead of telling me
i'm stupid
i'm crazy
i'm wrong
you comfort me
you see me

you hear me
my feelings are valid

we converse
about the rollercoaster
of emotions
and turmoil
braving the loops and plummets
instead of fearing
the journey altogether

you didn't realize how much that meant to me
but i didn't realize i was just a ride to you

four thousand five hundred and twenty nine miles

i sit
in a cafe
miles away
from you
and wonder
do you miss me too?

do you hear them now

i wrote you a short poem once
when you were to busy with life
to talk

it was a joke
it said

i am
upset
:(

you told me it was a great haiku

it's funny how you see the words
but don't count the syllables
or realize what i'm actually trying to say

you told me it wasn't as good as my other poems

how would you know
i never read them to you
you were always too busy with life to hear them

my heart breaks for you

you told me poetry was stupid
that you didn't get the point
that it was written too weirdly
phrased in an illogical way
expressing emotions too intimately

i told you that's the point
it's meant for you to look deeper
to find the hidden meaning
to let it speak to your soul

i told you i knew you wouldn't understand
because you had a hard time expressing emotions

and you told me i was wrong

you didn't struggle expressing emotions
you just didn't have any to express

different pages in different books

i lay alone in my bed
wishing you were here
while you're at the bar
happy i'm not there

a letter to him pt vi

you are the soul
that i could let see
into the depths
of mine

if i let myself
i could love you
with every fiber
every cell
in my body
it would be fierce
and passionate
and all-consuming
and comforting
and safe

you could be my home
and i could be yours

but
you don't want that
so i don't want that

i lock up my feelings
hidden from you
hidden from me
no possibility
of embracing them
because i know
the moment i do
they will come pouring out
tumbling through my lips
thundering in my ears
drowning the world out
like a tidal wave

please let me in

why are you like this?
who hurt you?
who has scarred your heart
so profoundly
that you are afraid to love

who has ruptured your soul
so unequivocally
that you locked it away
so deep
that not even you can find it

earthworms

you have burrowed your way into my heart
and made a home that will stay in me forever

we were never going to work

i feel too much
you feel nothing at all

a letter to him pt vii

regardless of the
swirling emotions
hidden from view
you understand my past
these walls have been built
for a reason
they did not come into fruition
of their own accords
they did not pick up the bricks themselves
and build their own foundation
they were not cemented together
by an invisible hand
they were built by many
hands that spread suffering
as easily as mortar between stones
hands that dealt unfathomable pain
and irreparable damage

supernova

i once thought our destiny
was written in the stars
but stars burn out

homesick

sometimes home can be a person
and you were mine

ungrateful

i come back
bloodied and bruised
open wounds
dripping blood
onto the dirt
as i walk
haphazard scars
cover my body
barely hidden under
my ragged shirt

you do not
ask me
what happened
     i fought for you
are you okay
     no
do you need help
     desperately
the first thing
you say is
why are you
bleeding on
my floor

a letter to him pt viii

i refuse to open the door
unlock the gate
lift the drawbridge
empty the moat

you
who could be my knight
in gleaming
glistening
shining armor

you
who could
but won't

you will never feel
my burning passion
the fierce desire
the swell in my heart
when your name
graces the lips of a stranger

these emotions are forbidden in your heart
they run from the cold
from the dying
from the rotten
and they find a home in mine

i will take care of them
until you repair your broken fissures
the drafty roof
the cracked windows
and leaky faucets
until you pull the weeds
clear the garden
plant the flowers
until you hammer the floorboards
sweep the wood
clean the doorframe

until then
i will keep them hidden
in the back of the shed
under a blanket
away from you

the grass is greener

he is here
smiling
bright
and bringing light
into my darkened world
    so why do i still want you

i still wear your bracelet

he tells me he cares
easily
without hesitation
he lets his feelings spill free
no barrier between his thoughts
and his words
he has no trouble
articulating exactly how he feels
about me
opening doors
giving unsolicited compliments
showing me off
buying me flowers

i never have to guess
where i stand with him

a letter to him pt ix

you told me you care
somewhere deep inside your psyche
i know you do
in your own way
but even then
belief does not come easily
to a heart that has been burned before

the actions of others
have broken your soul
you drift through relationships
in and out of doors
to places no one can ever follow

i shatter
when the realization strikes
that one day you will be grounded
one day someone will grasp your hand
and instead of feeling nothing but air
you will become solid and whole
you will return to the world of the living
and while i will rejoice at your unmutilated soul
flawless and unmarred and complete once again
my own soul will mourn
it will weep and grieve and wail
that i am not that someone

string hearts

if my soul
is truly attached to yours
we will come back together
when we are meant to be

if not
i will see you in another life

to you

rewriting rapunzel

when you feel alone
become strong for yourself

let others' opinions hit the brick wall
that you have built around your castle

and let them watch
as you build your tower high into the heavens

choices

the best advice
i ever received
was

"when one door closes
keep walking
until you find a window"

climb out the window
scrape your knees
get dirt on your clothes

and seize the world

a dish best served cold

there is no better revenge
than becoming exactly who
they didn't want you to be

apathy

i envy those in love
and those in heartbreak

i pity those who have never felt either

into the flames

what if i told you
that true love exists
but does not come
at first glance
or at first kiss

instead it comes
after you have been
to hell and back
together

selfish

never feel guilty for doing what is best for you
it means you are growing

right hook

never apologize for being who you are
you are special
you are exotic
you are gorgeous
you are your own person
you have your own thoughts
you have your own desires
you have your own destiny
and if anyone ever makes you feel
like you are less than you are
punch them in the face

open your eyes

isn't it interesting
how we can go
our whole lives
waiting to meet
the right person
only to find out
that the person
we needed
was inside of us
all along

forward thinking

your past may have
made you
created you
shaped you
but you cannot change it
or reverse time

your present can
make you
create you
shape you

you can make it
create it
shape it
change it

you write your future

playground cuts

you don't always need someone
to fix your soul
sometimes all you need
is to be your own band-aid

a letter to her

there are so many things
i wish i could tell
my younger self

first and foremost is:
getting him is never worth losing yourself
since i can't tell her i'll tell you

the lies we are told

why are we told
that a boy
pulling our hair
on the playground
means he likes us

doesn't this set us up for failure?

if we go through life
thinking that every boy
who is mean to us
who hurts us
harbors secret feelings

won't we miss the ones who actually care?

the curious circumstance of losing it all

it is an interesting feeling
hitting rock bottom
"there is
nowhere else
to go
but up"
they say
but what if
i just want
to lay down
and cry

i pity them

it is hard to write poetry when you don't acknowledge emotions

those who don't will never understand
the sheer relief you feel
when releasing all of the pent up energy
onto crisp clear new paper

they will never truly understand
the poems they read
they will want to change titles or lines or nuances
because "every line portrays the same emotion"
the subtleties will never click in their brain
the pictures will never paint themselves
the words will never speak to their soul

instead
all they
see are
intense
passionate
sentences
and they
will ask
themselves
"why does
the writer
care so
much"

harvest

it's a very curious sort of feeling
to realize that the world is in front of you
and that it's ripe for the taking

it's beautiful out here

it is easy to feel like an outsider
it is hard to make the outside
feel like home

the darkest before the dawn

after a night of crying into pillowcases about
broken promises
distraught emotions
shredded hearts
evaporated future plans

remember the dawn

with its golden rays
tangerine clouds
chilled breeze
and songbird chirps

is more refreshing than lemonade
on a hot summer day

romance doesn't use a watch

there is not such thing
as right person
wrong time
if it were the right person
time wouldn't matter

you are okay

when you see them
and no longer wonder
if they miss you

love is a beach

if sand was meant to stay in your hand
it wouldn't slip through your fingers
people are the same

i'd rather feel too much than nothing at all

isn't it
better
to wear
your heart
on your
sleeve
than
to not
have a
heart
at all

how to survive

it is fun
being empty
and heartless
giving hell
to the world
that made life
hell for you
      but that is not how you live

perspective

the first thought we think
is what we were taught
the second is what
we teach ourselves

fire and brimstone

i hope you never feel
the type of heartache
that fills you to the brim
with anger and hatred
and the utmost desire
to raze the world

but if you ever do
burn it to the ground

self-sufficient

there are no words
that i can use
to describe
the euphoric feeling
of standing up
for yourself
and not settling

it's climbing into the most comfortable bed
after the most arduous of days

it's biting into the softest cookie
fresh from the oven

it's a breath of the purest air
in the middle of a sunlit forest

it's taking back your own power
and realizing you are all you need

scarlet fever

red comes in hundreds of shades
spilled blood on the battlefield
plump cherries and the mouth that bites into them
merlot wine and cheese rinds
cut watermelons at a barbecue
valentines day hearts and smeared lipstick
autumn leaves as they litter the ground
bright raspberries in a picnic basket
bricks that build our homes
and stop signs and bloodshot eyes

it is the color of passionate love affairs
hidden away in hotel rooms
lust overpowering love
desire drowning out rationality

it is the color of vision
upon discovering betrayal
of pulsing blood
during confrontation
of flushed cheeks
during heated arguments
of storming out
and broken promises
and burning bridges

euphoria

the best feeling in the world
is when you realize
you are happy
without them

no answer is an answer

if they want you
you'll know

caring and trying are two different things

it does not matter
how difficult a relationship is

it could be the easiest in the world
and fall apart in the blink of an eye

what matters
is how much effort you put into it

willingly

if you have to
convince another person
to love you
for who you are
they're not worth it

the true meaning of a soulmate

you do not need someone
to complete you
your soul will survive
on its own

you only need someone
to accept you completely
wholeheartedly
and without reservations

adrenaline

it's an exhilarating feeling
to have absolutely no idea what you're doing

bottom line

you will never know what love feels like
until you learn to love yourself

to me

open and closed

horses gallop through open fields
birds fly through open skies
fish swim through open seas

i am trapped in my closed world

so i escape through poetry

poetry

it is hard to write a story
only using words and phrases
to paint a picture

it is harder still to write in a way
where those words and phrases
connect thousands of hearts

and it is damn near impossible to write in a way
that let those words and phases
heal your own soul as well

endothermic

i step into the sun
and open my eyes
feeling the warmth
on my face
on my body
warming everywhere
except my heart

the division of souls

isn't is strange
to find bits of myself
in others
to hear my words
in the mouths of friends
to watch my mannerisms
from across the room
and to realize
i have pieces of them
in me

stubbornness is a savior

you can try to douse the fire in my heart
shatter my self-confidence
disillusion everything i hold dear
but you will find yourself
fruitless in your endeavors
for you cannot kill my soul

cracks in my mirror

i am not afraid to say no
i tell the world my convictions strongly
never letting others' opinions sway my view
i wear my heart on my sleeve
express my emotions freely
and exude confidence in every step

i am afraid to say yes
to let the world into my heart
and to let you see every piece of me
to show what's beneath the surface
put my insecurities and doubts on display
and allow you to see through the cracks in my façade

letting someone in

i am standing on the edge
on the precipice of falling
staring into the abyss
as it stares back at me
taunting me
to jump

time to go to bed

do the people i love
love me the same way
do my friends
consider my a friend

biased

am i the same person
i think i am
when i look in the mirror

emotions do not fit in a box

am i in love or lust
am i empty or numb
am i happy or
am i just not sad

a scientific explantation

what if
we are soulmates
because when
the universe
was created
my atoms
were next
to yours
and they
have been
trying
to find
their way
back together
ever since

reflections can lie

the confidence is a façade
can you see through it
or do you see the mirror
i want you to see

shining bright

i no longer wonder
how long it will be
until i see the sun
for i know now
i am my own star

the absence of finality

i am used to
burned bridges
severed ties
communication cut off
no possibility to rekindle
no possibility i will be hurt
or hurt another

but to leave something open
i wonder

is it having hope for a future
or refusing to let go of the past

am i in the wrong century

what if
i no longer
want to
swipe right
or swipe left
what if
instead
i want to be
swept off
my feet

the diary of an overthinker

i feel things too deeply
every word
every silence
every gesture
can send me spiraling out of control

i analyze things too intensely
every look
every moment
every touch
can have me falling in love

my heart does not give second chances

i am a rare blossom
that only blooms
once in a lifetime

open heart surgery

i wear my heart of my sleeve proudly
let it bleed without reservations
it's not the repercussions that scare me
it's the idea of not loving at all

priceless

i now know my worth
i'll be damned if you make me forget it

hide and seek

i run
from the dark
from vulnerability
from talking to strangers
from answering the phone
from making appointments
from uncomfortable silences
and i hide under my covers
from awkward conversations
from navigating adulthood
from high expectations
from my emotions
from weird noises
from my trauma

i run and hide so much
i've lost how to find me

curiosity killed the cat

will i ever be content in this world
or will i always want more

i want to explore to the ends of the earth
and to climb to the snow-capped mountains

i want to cut through the dense jungle
and race across the savannah

i want to swim in the deepest ocean
and ride across the desert

my thirst for more is unquenchable
my wanderlust unrelenting

no place is safe from my prying
no culture from my passion

i am relentless in my endeavors
and thorough in my research
but satisfaction brought me back

snowballs

sometimes i wonder
what my soul is made of
what my presence feels like

is it like drinking hot chocolate with cinnamon while a fire burns
or watching bright bluebells sway in the summer breeze
or the sun shining thorough the clouds during a dreamy sunset

or is it like the comfort from the smell of rain
or dusty pages in an undisturbed antique bookshop
or the windy salt spray on your face from the ocean

am i the simple joy of biting into a warm and salted french fry
or walking down an empty parisian street with a fresh croissant
or the quiet stillness of an empty library at night

or am i a lazy sunday morning in bed
or a breath of fresh air in the autumn woods
or the euphoria of dancing to your favorite song

or am i none of these

do i feel like stale coffee at five am on a monday morning
or lost keys when you're rushing out the door
or stuffed noses in the dead of winter

is it freezing in the cold with bitter wind ripping through your coat
or burning your tongue and losing taste for the next three days
or running late to work and hitting every single red light on the way

am i your favorite pen running out of ink mid-sentence
or someone taking the last piece of cake you've been craving all day
or watching someone you love fall out of love with you
i don't know how i feel
but i know what others feel like

my mother feels like
coming home after being gone for years
only to find fresh cookies baking in the oven

my father feels like
the comfort of a crackling fireplace
and the intoxicating smell of burning wood

my best friend feels like
vodka shots and thanksgiving dinner
and midnight dives into the pool

but what do i feel like

i guess if i could choose
i would say i feel like
the childish glee of playing in the snow

evolution

i wonder what caterpillars go through
to come into this life
small and soft and easily hurt
knowing nothing of the future
or their purpose in life
only to enter a chrysalis
and emerge a butterfly

and then i think
don't we go through the same thing

a letter to me

i shine a spotlight on my demons
highlight my flaws
draw arrows to the cracks
circle the trauma
i will hide nothing from you
because if you can love me
after seeing all my flaws
my demons
my trauma
my broken parts
then i know
that you will love
the real me

i am free

from your bonds
from obligation
the world is mine to explore
this life is mine to live

notice

is it too much to ask
for somebody to notice me

to notice
that i don't drink coffee
but tea with honey and lemon
that i brush my hair out of my face
then move it back
because i hate the way it makes me look
that i twist my rings
around my fingers
when i'm nervous or bored
that i prefer to write
in pen rather then pencil
and watch the ink sink into the pages

to notice
when i am okay
and when i am not

i don't need a knight

to hell with the world
i will write my own story
slay my own dragons
and forge my own destiny

middle ground

i find it so easy
to write down
my emotions
into lines
and stanzas

here on paper
they are safe
i don't have to face
the consequences
of my words spoken aloud

i don't have to be brave
but still i think
that i am not a coward
because i am brave enough
to feel them at all

revelation

the best moment in my life
was when i realized
i am enough

i was never going to make it out alive

i return home from war
not holding my shield
but on it
i have lost it all
i died for something that was
doomed from the start

from the ashes

i have been beaten down
bloodied and bruised
i have had my soul obliterated
my heart hardened
and the light inside of me
extinguished

this is not my heroic reentrance
into the world
    this is my villain origin story

sonder

i wonder
are their lives
filled with the epic love stories
the highs and lows
that i experience

or

are my experiences
trivial in comparison
to their grand exploits

or

is my life the fascination

sometimes i wonder who i would be
if i wasn't me
if i wasn't the student
the daughter
the writer
that i am

what life would i live?

would i be an archeologist
discovering humanity's past
covered in dirt day after day
uncovering fossils and artifacts

would i be a model
walking the runway in milan
famous for my beauty
yet always criticized

would i be a chef
creating fantastical dishes
that tempt the taste buds
and delight the senses

would i be a fashion designer
sketching the new and exciting
dealing with fame and madness
and revolutionizing the world

would i be a singer
and have thousands of fans
all around the world
screaming my name

would i be a marine biologist
scuba diving with sharks
documenting changes
in multicolored reefs

would i be a ceo
who puts the dreams
i have on the shelf
to stockpile money instead

would i own a bookshop
or a flower shop
and romanticize
my life in rural europe

or would i be exactly where i am now
i like to think i would

thank you

to my amazing editor aly, who i would have been completely lost without

to maddy for being my absolute best friend since 6th grade and supporting me through this

to garrett who was a greater inspiration than he will ever know

to my lovely beta readers, ellie, edie, sophie, and elle

to john for being my first ever rejection and telling me that i would never get this published

to caroline for sitting with me in a park for hours working on the perfect titles

to the city of paris for inspiring me to start writing again

and finally to my parents for being my biggest support system throughout my entire life and for always encouraging me to chase my dreams and never give up

jamie papazis is a 20 year old college student currently attending the university of alabama. her first published work, *the letters we write,* received high praise for her raw and honest poetry and blunt reminder of what it means to go through heartbreak and to return stronger for it. when she's not on campus, she's in her apartment reading, cooking, and taking care of her two kittens.